SPIRIT OF BUSINESS

A Leadership Guide For The New Capitalist Era

George T. Johnson

INTRODUCTION

90% of the business leaders of today believe that an engagement strategy has a beneficial effect on the success of the company.

However, just 25% of them have a strategy for putting this into action.

Your people are the source of your competitive advantage in today's environment of intense competition. When it comes to employee activation, outdated corporate methods and training programs that involve "information dumping" are no longer adequate. The rules have been altered. Have you altered your strategy to compete?

Table of contents

Chapter 1: **MEANING OF WORK**

What is work?

Work is any activity requiring mental or physical effort carried out in pursuit of a goal or outcome.

It is an employment-related mental or physical activity that generates income.

a location or set of facilities used for industrial or manufacturing processes.

ADAM'S CURSE

The story "Adam's Curse" examines the concept that people have to work very hard in order to achieve beauty in their lives, especially in their art and their romantic relationships. The speaker of the poem argues that writing poetry is much more difficult than it first appears to be while conversing with two other female companions, one of whom is his unrequited love interest and the other is her friend. When the "friend" reminds him that ladies are aware that all beauty involves "labour," the speaker responds that love was once considered hard work as well. This is a veiled barb at the woman who has not been moved by any of the speaker's attempts at romance. The poem makes the suggestion, tinged with a bittersweet melancholy, that creating art, appreciating beauty, and being in love are all sorts of laborious work that are not guaranteed to be valued in the end. The speaker contends that they are frequently a form of martyrdom: the heroic effort that is put into them may only be returned with sorrow on the part of the recipient.

The poem makes the case that writing poetry is a significantly more challenging endeavour than the general public realises. The speaker, who is standing in for the poet himself, explains (or maybe complains) that individual lines of poetry can take hours of work, but in the end, the poem as a whole needs to sound effortless, or else it was all for nothing. In addition to this, he asserts that the work of poets is more difficult than that of manual labour, despite the general public's perception that poets are lazy. To put it another way, the fact that skilled poets can make it appear effortless leads others to believe that it is effortless, or even instinctive and natural.

This same approach is extended to beauty and love in the conversation that takes place between the speaker and the "close friend." That is to say, neither of these things comes naturally, and accomplishing each one of them takes a lot of hard work. Following the speaker's discussion of poetry, the companion responds by asserting that every woman is aware that "we must work to be attractive." To put it another way, an effort is required to create any form of beauty, not only the literary variety. The speaker alludes to the biblical curse that was placed on Adam, which required him and all men to "toil" in order to survive. The speaker then gives a pointed reply by saying that lovers used to put a lot of effort into courting one another, but that this practice appears to have fallen out of favor in recent years. The inference is that the woman he "strove" to win has rejected his arduous courtship; this is most likely in favor of someone who did not court her as seriously as he did.

As a result of the speaker's disappointment, it is now possible to consider the idea that the "labor" of art, beauty, and love may never be gratifying in any conventional sense. Work of this nature is, at its best, a selfless but exhausting sacrifice. The speaker remarks in a sarcastic tone that love in and of itself appears to be an "idle trade" nowadays, where "idle" can signify either laziness or insignificance.

It appears as though the effort and larger purpose that he had previously associated with it have been lost. In an earlier section of the poem, he made a comparison between poets and what he called "the martyrs calling the world," which refers to individuals who work in the world of everyday life, practical matters, and transactional activities. But now, as the poem draws to a close, this contrast shows that those who work in support of art, beauty, and love are themselves "martyrs," which is a term referring to idealists who give themselves for their ideas.

WHY WE WORK

Why We Work investigates the role that works plays in our lives by looking at how various people regard their jobs, what characteristics contribute to a sense that one's work has significance, and what questions businesses should ask in order to get the most out of their employees in terms of motivation.

The reasons why people go to work can provide us with valuable insight into their experiences while they are there.

Some people just view their job as a means to an end; they go to work in order to put food on the table, pay their rent or mortgage, and provide for themselves and their families, including treating themselves to occasional treats or indulgences. They are obligated to work, but you shouldn't expect them to go above and beyond the basic requirements of their position.

Some people look at their job as their career and view their ascent up the corporate ladder as an opportunity for personal development and professional advancement. This is evidenced by promotions, increases in compensation, and increased levels of responsibility. These individuals have a propensity to view their employment as something more than just a job and anticipate receiving a great deal more satisfaction from what they do.

For other people, their job is a calling; they see it as a means of bringing about positive change in the world as well as a source of satisfaction for themselves.

Some people engage in labor to earn a living. They require funds to purchase food, pay their rent, and have fun with their loved ones and friends. Independence.

MOTIVATING FACTORS THAT DRIVE US TO WORK TREMENDOUSLY

In reality, the only three factors that consistently motivate the majority of us to put in long hours of labor are:

1. **MONEY**: To earn money, people labor hard. They require money to pay their rent, buy food, and enjoy themselves with their loved ones.

2. **INDEPENDENCE**: Working is not simply done for financial gain. Additionally, having a job might help you feel more independent and in charge of your own life. Working allows you to gain new knowledge, develop your existing talents, and develop friendships with coworkers.

3. **THE COMMUNITY**: People put in effort to participate in and support their communities. This implies that tasks are not only for your advantage; they also enable you to assist others. Let's imagine, for illustration, that I deliver mail at work. I'm assisting the entire workplace in getting things done and saving time.

EACH AND EVERYDAY ISSUE WITH PERFECTION

After all, striving for perfection is ultimately a futile way to navigate the world. It is based on the painful irony that making errors and owning up to them is an essential component of learning, developing, and being a human. You get better in your job, your relationships, and life in general as a result of it. Perfectionists can make it more difficult to accomplish their lofty objectives by avoiding mistakes at all costs.

The disadvantage of perfectionism, however, goes beyond the fact that it prevents you from being your most effective and successful self. A long list of clinical conditions has been linked to perfectionism, including depression, anxiety, self-harm, social anxiety disorder, agoraphobia, binge eating, anorexia, bulimia, and other eating disorders, post-traumatic stress disorder, chronic fatigue syndrome, insomnia, hoarding, dyspepsia, chronic headaches, and, most damning of all, even early mortality and suicide.

High standards are not what perfectionism is about. It has to do with irrational standards. Being perfect is not a behavior. It's a way of approaching yourself.

Perfectionism can be harmful as well. The World Health Organization reports that young people are experiencing mental illness in record proportions. In comparison to a decade ago, depression, anxiety, and suicidal thoughts are more prevalent in the US, Canada, and the UK today. Even when researchers took into account personality qualities like neuroticism, evidence demonstrates that perfectionistic impulses predict problems like melancholy, anxiety, and stress. Making matters worse, having negative thoughts about oneself may trigger depressed symptoms, which may in turn exacerbate negative thoughts about oneself, creating a distressing cycle.

Perfectionism is not the only thing that leads to mental health issues; some of these issues themselves can lead to perfectionism. For instance, a recent study indicated that college students with social anxiety were more likely to develop into perfectionists over a year, but not the other way around.

It has also been demonstrated that self-compassion, which perfectionists lack, is one of the strongest defenses against anxiety and despair. Additionally, sadness is predicted by the perfectionists' propensity for self-criticism.

Chapter 2: THE PURPOSEFUL HUMAN ORGANIZATION

Organization, according to King Dino, is a setting where regular people may accomplish extraordinary things. One of the most important aspects of purpose is that it makes it clear why an organization exists. From a customer, social, and economic perspective, who does it intend to affect? What makes people want to join the organization and engage with its mission is what draws them to its vision. When it comes to luring talent to your firm, your purpose is also a crucial differentiation. What draws people to careers in government? Why do they work in healthcare, and for what reasons? What makes them desire to work for your company? One of the crucial differentiators you can use to draw in top people and enable them to connect with your organization's mission and provide excellent results for your clients, society, and the economic goals you're trying to promote. Unfortunately, most organizations don't provide us with very good responses when we ask them what the objective of their company is. Frequently, we do receive the response, but it's all for financial gain. How inspiring is that for your staff?. Your consumers, employees, and products are your main constituents. Unfortunately, the majority of senior executives are shackled by their narrow perspectives. always considering the upcoming quarter and the subsequent minor accomplishment. The company will be viewed as a failure if they are unable to meet those expectations with the markets. This causes us to become stuck in our short-term thinking and lose the vision and purpose for which the business was initially formed. Many organizations have been seen to lose sight of their goals. with time they lose their meaning. And frequently, this might be one of the first signs that a business is likely to fail. Businesses cease imagining big. They begin to believe that dreaming big is merely creating the newest mobile application. It's not a major deal for businesses.

People are being urged to consider the clarity, the purpose, and the vision of building outstanding companies that people want to be a part of, feel connected to and feel like they can understand their contribution and how it's achieving that mission and purpose at the business.

Leaders like Elon Musk are renowned for having lofty goals and being incredibly demanding of their teams. They exert a lot of pressure on them to realize such goals. However, they thrive in concentrating on outlining what matters to the company. They push their teams hard but have faith that their employees will find out how to get there. Because they are aware that there would be numerous challenges to overcome when pursuing an ambitious objective or vision. Their objective is to identify these barriers as soon as possible and come up with fun, fresh solutions to overcome them. They understand that part of their job as a leader is to keep the company's goals in mind and to be willing to collaborate with their teams as they devise strategies to achieve them. What is the goal of your company? Can you put it in writing? Does everyone in your company comprehend what it is there to accomplish? How do you believe you advance the goals of your company? Is it evident? What would your organization's purpose be if you could put it in writing? Get your team together in a cross-functional group to attempt and figure out what the goal of your company is. What is the goal of the project you're engaged in? How can you concentrate on expressing that to others in a clear manner? So they are aware of the significance of this and what needs to be accomplished.

THE CONTROL OF SHAREHOLDER'S VALUE

The Interest that an individual shareholder receives as a result of owning shares in a corporation is referred to as shareholder value.

The term "Control of Shareholder Values" refers to a system in which an organization has complete decision-making power and dominates all facets of shareholder rights, to the point where the rights and values of shareholders are disregarded.

The perspective that places the corporation first is an improved alternative principle. It is the fact that the continued existence of the corporation itself is the corporation's ultimate goal in existence. It is not the responsibility of the company to look out for the best interests of its shareholders, employees, vendors, the environment, or anybody else or anything else. The Costco business model is analyzed here.

THE BUSINESS OF BUILDING A CATHEDRAL

Shareholder value or return on investment are not factors in the Law of Building a Cathedral. These are, in a way, insignificant in the context of what your company stands for. I say this not because I think it, but because so few of your employees will ever be genuinely motivated by the desire to boost operating profits.

It's about having a personal connection to the organization's mission, vision, and goals. It kind of supplants who you are and what you want to be. As they spend more time working with you, your direct reports and colleagues also realize how important their work is to the mission. They believe they are crucial to its success, and this belief motivates them and instills in them a sense of accountability and trust.

In order to be truly effective, executives must find the mission that all employees will "understand" and offer it as their cathedral building project, not as a document articulating the strategic vision or as a meaningless Mission Statement that is laminated, tacked to the wall, and generally ignored. Beyond simply delivering it, they must constantly live it, and they must expect each leader in the organization to persuade everyone in their sphere of influence to do the same.

The Mission: It is not original. Instead, it is learned within the organization or transmitted from a superior power outside the organization. The Mission from God inspires people by linking the job that takes up our days with a purpose greater than ourselves, as opposed to what used to be called a Big Hairy Audacious Goal (BHAG), which tries to motivate by the size of the goal. Even if the job isn't very fulfilling, this aim might inspire someone to produce excellent work.

The Power of Vision: The reason why vision is so potent is that, when we have a clear vision, we can practically reverse-engineer our reality using the blueprints of that vision.

I feel as though I am no longer able to give counsel to others who approach me for it after becoming more aware of my vision and spending some time developing my own "vision plan."

The realization that so few people have life visions astounds me. Most people are content to simply lay bricks. A cathedral is being built by a very small group of people.

Although many people have objectives, aspirations, and dreams, only a small number have a clear vision. The vision has several advantages over transactional objectives, irrational aspirations, and passive fantasies.

My preference for a vision plan over any of the above is based on the fact that a vision may be translated into daily practical steps.

Goals: goals are frequently one-dimensional, hopes are reserved for the helpless, and dreams are held only by dreamers. A powerful idea that has been translated into manageable daily actions, however, is unstoppable.

The world may be altered one "brick" at a time by having a compelling vision, translating that vision into a blueprint, then following the modest, doable actions in the blueprint.

The future belongs to those of us who have clear goals, detailed plans for accomplishing those goals, and a detailed schedule of daily doable tasks.

The Organization: Any group of people or society established by the Dean or the Cathedral Wardens is considered an organization if they work effectively to ensure that things are done correctly for the benefit of everybody.

Are you putting bricks or constructing a temple in your life right now?

Which cathedral are you constructing? It's yours? or that of someone else?

WORKING WITH A DECENT PERSON

This also applies to permanent employees, staff, managers, department heads, and supervisors. Not many of us who work do so with a noble heart.

Everyone wants to feel important in what they do. Everyone longs for a cause.

Being a man of noble workmanship involves both what you do and how you do it, The sense of purpose, significance, and grandeur that we all want can be provided by a worker with a noble heart.

Here are a few of the methods they employ:

1. **An employee with a noble heart makes us feel important**:

Everyone puts out more effort when they believe they are having an impact. The desire to feel that our work matters, to develop and increase our abilities, and to live and work purposefully are all addressed by noble workmanship.

2. **We receive a noble sense of moral support from a decent worker**: Noble craftsmanship is not about the self; rather, it is about helping, leading, and attending to the needs of others while also bringing out the best in them.

3. **We are given a noble sense of honor by a decent worker**: The key to everything and what enables us to achieve greatness is a feeling of honor. Noble craftsmanship is founded on honor and encourages others to uphold honor.

4. **A decent worker inspires us with a good spirit.** People ache to contribute to something greater than themselves. A noble worker motivates others by making them feel important, which incites a desire to work more.

5. **A decent worker makes us feel good about ourselves**. You are much more driven and inclined to keep moving in the right way when you are visible and being seen. Decent workers are aware of the value of visibility

and that hiding from view is the surest way to feel inadequate.

6. **Workmanship**: workmanship has the potential to become our most important resource; the caliber of the workforce determines whether or not new developments take place. When we lead with a noble heart, that will be the turning point. This doesn't imply that you are out there trying to save the world, but rather that you are letting every person you come into contact with know that they matter.

7. **Lead From Within**: Learn how to be like the manager who works with a team and recognizes their contributions, the boss who sacrifices their pleasures to provide more for their employees, and the employee who sacrifices their own life to improve the lives of their clients. These are the people who work with a noble heart.

HOW TO RESTRUCTURE YOUR COMPANY USING THE PERSONNEL YOU ALREADY HAVE

CEOs can save a failing company by using the personnel they already have. All that is needed is a management strategy that unleashes the organization's full potential.

Many turnaround initiatives start by removing the existing team and bringing in a new one. This is the organization that oversaw the downturn, so it makes sense. But there are times when clearing the decks is not an option. The company's past can get in the way. The atmosphere outside might prevent it. There can be other restrictions.

That isn't necessarily a problem because CEOs can save a failing company by using the personnel they already have. All that is needed is a management strategy that unleashes the organization's full potential.

Any CEO or top executive wishing to replicate these positive outcomes should begin with these 6 crucial actions.

1. Define the issue
2. Identify the core problems affecting the company quickly,
3. Clearly define your goals,

4. Create a clear vision of the organization's future through working with the organization,
5. Give authority to the group that will carry out the work, Make it clear that the team is free to act however they like. After that,
6. Take a step back, Stay away from interfering and undermining team members. Instead, make an effort to get rid of any obstacles.

The four main priorities of Agile management are often shared by businesses that do a good job of empowering their employees,

1. People and relationships over procedures and equipment:

People are what adapt to and strive to satisfy company needs. When they are held in high regard, they might be more adaptable and productive.

2. Working software over thorough documentation, Employees can concentrate on the task at hand when paperwork is simplified.
3. Collaboration with the client during contract negotiations makes customers a continuing part of the process rather than just negotiating with them at the beginning. The likelihood of their demands being addressed will thus be significantly increased.

4. Adapting to change but still sticking to a plan. Change should not be avoided or disregarded. It enhances a project and presents an opportunity to offer clients more value.

You will likely need to work with those who are currently in the trenches to fix an underperforming company if you join it. What will you do with the team you have then?

Chapter 3: UNLEASHING HUMAN MAGIC

This entails bringing forth a person's enormous potential for their line of work. Individuals have typically been motivated in corporations using a combination of carrots and sticks: a system of financial incentives intended to rally everyone around a plan created by a small group of intelligent people at the top. Financial benefits do not motivate people to work more or perform better for any task requiring cognitive or creative talents, according to numerous research. What does, then? Hubert Joly, the former CEO of Best Buy, asserts that several interdependent factors must come together to foster the kind of human magic required for a company's purpose to take hold and grow. He offers six elements to make the special batch of human magic your business uses.

THE CARROTS AND STICK METHOD

The traditional theory of motivation known as the "Carrot and Stick Method" contends that in order to get people to behave in a certain way, rewards are sometimes given in the form of money, promotions, or other financial or non-financial benefits, and punishments are other times used to push people in that direction.

The Carrot and Stick method of motivation is based on the concepts of reinforcement and was developed during the industrial revolution by the philosopher Jeremy Bentham. According to this notion, the easiest method to get a donkey moving is to hold a carrot in front of him and poke him with a stick from behind. The stick is used to punish him for not moving while the carrot is used to encourage him to move.

As a result, when someone performs well, they receive a carrot or reward, and when they don't, they receive a stick or punishment. The following things must be taken into consideration when administering punishments:

1. If a person chooses desirable alternative conduct, punishment is said to be successful in changing the behavior.

2. The conduct will be momentarily restrained and may reemerge after the punishment has ended if the aforementioned requirement is not met.
3. When the penalty is administered right after the unwanted activity, it has a greater impact.
4. The management must ensure that the punishment is applied correctly and does not serve as a reward for the improper behavior.

The carrot and stick method of motivation should therefore be used with care so that both have a motivating impact on the employees of the firm.

First Component: CONNECTING DREAMS AND MINDSET

Stories and pictures that our imaginations conjure up while we sleep are known as dreams. They can be humorous, enjoyable, romantic, upsetting, frightful, and even weird.

Connecting Dreams:

The idea of a link in a dream represents the bringing together of opposites and the new energy that results from it. On the other side, the link in the dream represents the goals of a group unification that will benefit everyone. Most of the time, a connection with others denotes a desire for a romantic relationship.

The collaborative, equitable, and responsible aspects of the connected dream are sought after and emphasized. As the lessons on Connectors demonstrate, even amid violent conflicts, people work together and show concern for one another; certain ideologies and institutions serve to unite rather than divide people.

Failure is inevitable, especially at the beginning of any connecting campaign, therefore success is the result of failure. By letting go of your fear of being rejected and embracing the curiosity that is within, you can develop your connection attitude. Too many people abandon excellent connection strategies when they don't get immediate results.

You must set yourself apart from the rest of your industry at this point. If you think you have a good concept that works for you, test it out, track its effectiveness, and refine it until you receive the desired outcomes.

You've made connection errors in the past, and you'll continue to do so if you're like everyone else who has ever launched a job or business. If you can develop the correct mindset, this could be beneficial for your company.

Examine the best outcomes you've been able to achieve in terms of growing your connection network in the previous 12 months. It's probably not the result of some wild notion you put into action in 30 minutes. It was presumably a concept that was built upon another concept that you had successfully used in the past. Testing, evaluating, and improving your capacity to relate to your potential clients takes time.

Most likely, you took a typical connection, made it better in some way, and converted a client into a fan.

In that case, you have developed a connection mentality.

How could I improve this relationship, you wondered yourself. And this straightforward query helped you succeed.

You might be found and connected to people in various ways. Some clients came to you after being recommended by friends, while others discovered you online by searching for assistance and finding you under the correct keywords.

Each method creates a weak link, and it is up to you to discover ways to strengthen it.

I believe that developing connections requires seven steps. Although each step is significant, I think that step #6 is perhaps the most significant.

1. **Examine previous outreach strategies:**
Going to conferences and writing wonderful letters to your target customers have both been successful moves in the past for your career and business. You've used your linking superpowers to your advantage to attain this success (passion, focus, and strengths).
 Why did these connection methods previously work for you?
You can start developing your linking superpowers if you can respond to this query.

2. **Ask yourself, "What could I do to strengthen my capacity for interpersonal connection?":**
This is fantastic since it means that you have some connecting tricks up your sleeve. The next stage is to refine these methods so you can achieve better outcomes.
 Say you have a conference the following week. Perhaps you excel at igniting conversations but struggle with follow-up.
What could you do to increase the enjoyment of the situation for both you and your contact?

You might give them a token of your appreciation along with a $5 Starbucks gift card and a printout of one of your most well-liked articles. Or perhaps request an interview from them for your podcast. Consider various concepts and gauge their viability.

3. **Decide on the candidate with the most values and interest**:

After brainstorming several ideas, especially if you're straying from your usual methods of interaction, you need to choose the one that will yield the most return on investment.

The return on investment (ROI) I'm referring to includes both your financial investment and how much you value connecting with others. The majority of my clients fall short in this area. Instead of connecting from a place that makes them happy, they connect in a way that they believe would be successful (marketing).

I prefer to refer to this as "heart bonding." You make the process more enjoyable for both you and your possible new customer when you inject your personality into it.

4. **Develop a hypothesis**.

What do you anticipate will occur when you use this connection concept?

Consider that you would like to make 50 to 100 respectable contacts while attending a conference with 2,000 other attendees.

Consider that you test your connection plan after receiving 63. You send them a thank-you note, a Starbucks gift card, and an article you believe will help them appreciate and understand your company.

What will happen in response? How do you intend to follow up?

5. **Put the theory into practice**.

The next stage is to set up everything so that this method may be implemented quickly. Consider how you'll collect data from folks. What will you do to help them remember you?

Will, you pre-purchase the "thank you" cards? What could you do to make everything so simple that all you would have to do when you got back to the office was put your plan into action?

then simply take action.

6. **Monitor the outcomes.**

Let's say you spend $1,000 setting up and implementing this idea, and 10 people get back to you or your follow-up email. One of these 10 individuals pays $3,000 to become a client. Then, your ROI is favorable. Without accounting for your time, you have earned $2,000 in profit.

You'll start to notice a pattern if you try this again and manage to land two clients for $2,000 each.

7. **The decision to abandon or improve a concept is the last step**.

Keep in mind that most ideas typically don't function properly right away. However, after you have some data, you may determine whether to abandon it or improve it.

Depending on your connection campaign's reach, I advise trying an idea at least five times or for five months before giving up. For instance, you can't advertise for a month and hope to get a lot of connections out of it. You must give it some time. Building your connections requires being consistent.

The Second component: ESTABLISHING HUMAN CONNECTION

That human interaction may have such a profound impact is not surprising. Consider a person who made a significant impact on your life. Did you like them because they were intelligent? because their credentials were the strongest? since they had a pleasant scent? No, it was probably because you thought they were concerned about you.

Connection happens at that point because we become receptive to learning from others when we sense that they are concerned about us. The fact that many of us carry significant baggage that prevents us from caring about the people we encounter is another factor in why we can't relate to others. We carry around our modesty, skepticism, competition, and pride. However, things don't have to be this way. Sean made several important discoveries when interacting with some of the most compelling leaders in the world. These 13 fundamental methods may be used to connect with just about anyone.

Maslow's Hierarchy of Wants states that, in addition to food, water, and safety, the most crucial needs we must satisfy are love and belonging. This encompasses our desire for closeness with others, intimacy, social interaction, and group integration. We feel better overall and have happier lives when these requirements are satisfied.

Additionally, interacting with others reduces health risks and increases longevity as well as physical wellness. Strong social ties improve your chances of living longer by 50% and boost your immune system.

How do you interact with people? Six strategies to feel more bonded

Being daring and taking risks is sometimes necessary to establish interpersonal bonds. For instance, starting a conversation with a stranger can be frightening, particularly if you're shy. Even though you might feel anxious, you must push yourself to leave your comfort zone.

In the end, the satisfying sensation of making new friends much overcomes any initial apprehension you may experience when putting yourself out there. Let's examine six straightforward methods for assimilating into society.

1. **Spend time with others who share your interests**:

Getting along with folks who have similar interests and pastimes to you is simple.

If you enjoy reading, joining a book club can be a wonderful opportunity to meet others who have the same interests as you and make new friends.

Another option is to join a local running club if you enjoy staying active and meeting new people.

2. **Get through your obstacles**:

Because we all naturally dread rejection, developing relationships can be scary. But in order to form these connections, we need to get over our aversion to change and accept circumstances that are uncomfortable for us.

3. **Smiling (sometimes) and adopting a pleasant outlook**:

Initial impressions matter. Attempting to maintain a generally upbeat attitude and a genuine grin will automatically attract others. This does not need you to always be upbeat or uncritically hopeful. However, it's beneficial to practice appreciation and spend a few minutes reflecting on the positive aspects of your life before interacting with people. According to research, when it comes to making social connections, people are more drawn to good emotions than to negative ones.

Put your best self forward to increase your chances of being a people magnet.

4. **Be honest with others:**

Allow yourself to be more open and vulnerable with others if you want to establish friends more quickly. That does not imply that all filters or boundaries should be removed. Too much, too soon might alienate people and make you feel more isolated. However, you are not required to be a polished version of yourself.

Let them see the most honest version of you since people can tell when someone is being sincere or not. Additionally, they will feel at ease with you and establish a deeper connection with you as a result of your vulnerability.

5. **Don't stay engrossed in your phone**:

When we're uneasy in a social setting, it's simple to hide in our smartphones. However, this may make it harder for us to connect with others in real life.

For instance, using your phone while networking or attending a party will make you seem unapproachable. When you're out and about, put your attention on being present and interacting with those around you.

6. **Maintain contact**:

The bonds between people must be fostered. As an illustration, if you've made a new buddy, stay in touch with them and strengthen your bond. Work on preserving your current connections with close friends, family, or coworkers at the same time.

Regular communication strengthens relationships and makes sure you don't lose touch with the people you value most

Third component: FOSTERING AUTONOMY

What is AUTONOMY?

In a firm or business, autonomy refers to the discretion that managers grant staff members while making decisions and achieving specific goals. This could promote commitment to various roles and duties as well as job satisfaction. At different levels of an organization, including employees, supervisors, and teams, you can frequently discover specific sorts of autonomy. These kinds of autonomy frequently contribute to excellent outcomes for the entire business and boost overall productivity.

Managerial Autonomy

Giving managers more freedom typically enables them to make important personnel choices and may even enable them to reward or recognize workers without seeking management permission. Managers may be able to participate more actively in the growth of the organization and feel more engaged in important corporate decisions as a result. When leaders give managers autonomy, it can have a significant positive impact on their motivation and confidence levels, just like it does for employees.

Employee Independence

Through their projects and assignments, managers and executives frequently provide their staff members autonomy, allowing them to choose the most effective strategy for achieving the project's objectives. Employees can then concentrate on the development of their innate abilities while feeling empowered and inspired to accomplish a good job at their jobs as a result.

How to promote an autonomous culture in your company

Here is a list of actions you can take to foster your workplace's autonomy:

1. **Comprehending various viewpoints**:

Employees might not be as excited about some tasks as they are about others, such as redoing work or rectifying errors. When this happens, it can be helpful for managers to acknowledge the employee's attitudes, reaffirm the project's main aims or objectives, and discuss strategies for achieving those goals with the person. Employees will be better able to appreciate the need for the task, work with managers to discover solutions, and become more enthusiastic about the job as a result.

2. **Support employee passions**:

It can be helpful for managers to assign projects that employees can be passionate about by encouraging staff to let management know about their main interests or areas of enthusiasm. Employee autonomy and commitment to addressing complex challenges and producing results can both be enhanced by fostering passion. For instance, if a manager is aware of a worker's love of learning chances, giving them fresh challenges can keep them engaged in their work and even inspire them to go above and beyond what is expected of them by the employer.

3. **Provide employees with chances to exercise initiative:**

Giving workers the chance to exercise initiative and become more independent can boost their sense of independence and allow them to develop their professional abilities. This frequently helps the business as a whole, producing high-quality outputs for clients and inspiring other staff members to take initiative too. Consider giving employees the assignment's goals and providing them with a few broad rules to assist them to achieve while attempting to offer them more independence. This gives individuals the option to obey the rules or develop their strategy for reaching the goal.

4. **Supply the appropriate equipment for the work**:

When attempting to improve autonomy, it can be beneficial to make sure that workers have the proper equipment and resources at their disposal to finish their work. Giving employees the tools they need to succeed, whether that entails crucial software, extra team members, or further training, can help them understand that the business trusts them to complete the job but is still able and willing to support them in any way can.

5. **Establish limits for particular decisions:**
Setting restrictions on employees' freedom can be advantageous for a business or organization that is just beginning to make its process more independent. As a result, employees may be able to gradually move to a more self-managed role while maintaining achieving objectives and providing clients with goods or services.

For instance, if a manager wishes to give a worker greater freedom, they can assign them a project and let them finish it in any way they see fit, as long as it satisfies all of the client's given requirements. This can allow the worker to complete the task in their manner while still producing high-quality outcomes.

6. **Understand how to handle errors**:
In a work environment where there is more independence for employees, occasional blunders are likely. To continue fostering an employee's autonomy, supervisors and executives may find it crucial to tackle mistakes in a supportive and encouraging way. This may entail figuring out how the error was made, resolving the problem, and speaking with the employee so they are aware of how to avoid the error in the future. The person can

then be given more freedom while still being periodically checked on to see whether they've learned anything new or improved.

7. **Promote work-life harmony**:

Encouragement of a healthy balance between work and personal duties might occasionally aid people in understanding their limits and boost productivity. Because of the designated intervals for rest and recuperation, employees frequently boost their focus and efficiency during working hours when work and personal time are separated. Employee productivity can be increased and important communication skills can be developed by allowing them the opportunity to set limits and prioritize their personal lives.

8. **Consistently communicate**:

When providing employees more liberty, constant communication with them might be crucial. Then, managers may check in on how their staff members are doing and determine whether they need or want any assistance with their tasks. This provides them the chance to work together or continue honing their problem-solving abilities independently, and it can demonstrate to them that the organization has a robust support structure for its employees.

Fourth component: REALIZING DREAMS

There's no reason why life has to feel like an unending series of difficulties. People frequently struggle to reach their objectives because they lack a clear understanding of what they want. You may successfully traverse life's problems and truly make a difference for the better by using these five straightforward methods to manifest your aspirations and goals.

1. **Set definite goals for yourself**: The issue with most people is frequently that they are unsure of what they want out of life. They are aware that they desire lavish trips and quality time with their families, but they are unsure about how they intend to get there. When you are unclear about what you want, you leave yourself vulnerable to detours and, more importantly, inaction. Be as specific as you can while defining your life's goals. If you want a job in a bank, make a note of it and visualize yourself doing it. It may seem absurd, but you won't act without belief to move forward. More

action is taken toward what you genuinely want as you get more explicit.

2. **Write Down Your Goals And Keep Them Visible**:

Once you have a firm understanding of your objectives, write them down and keep them visible. Make sure to maintain your list in a location where you have to refer to it frequently, if necessary. Also, check items off your list when you accomplish your objectives. Although it may initially seem as though nothing is getting done, gradually you'll start crossing things off of that list, which will keep you motivated. It will be simpler for you to concentrate on your goals if you keep them in plain sight. This will keep them at the forefront of your thoughts. If you can't see your goals, you'll lose sight of them and stop paying attention to them, which will result in inaction. Keep your dreams and goals prominent and at the forefront of your mind as frequently as you can if you're serious about realizing your potential.

3. **Overcome Your Fear**:

Nothing stops you in your tracks like fear. Reactions to fear, as well as reactions to the terror of what hasn't happened yet, form a significant portion of human existence. Give up allowing fear to rule your life. Worrying about potential outcomes keeps you in a potential future; worrying about potential outcomes of past events keeps you in a world that you can no longer control. Live in the moment and concentrate on the things that make you happy and motivate you. When you become aware that your fear is preventing you from accomplishing your goals, take a moment to stop and tell yourself that this is just your fear of talking and that nothing horrible is occurring to you right at this moment. Repeat this as often as required. Remind yourself of all the positive aspects of your life and the fact that everything is okay right now. Do what needs to be done and don't let fear stop you from being who you are since life is only enjoyed in the now.

4. **Surround Yourself With Positive People:**
It's time to unplug from the internet and cable. It's time to let go of the activities you engage in during the day if they aren't helping you achieve your clearly stated objectives. Even though they might be entertaining, television, movies, and the internet can also serve as life avoidance tools and distractions. You can protest, "I have no time!" but what are you doing with your downtime? If after

work you discover that you come home, eat supper, and then spend the remaining hours of the day engaging in useless activities before going to bed, you should have a clear understanding of why your goals aren't being met. You don't have to give up all of your mindless entertainment, but if it consumes your entire life outside of work, you may want to consider how much time you're spending with friends and other useless activities. Look at your friend network. Are there individuals there who help you grow, or are people there who keep you rooted in the same, unchanging place? It might be time to cut ties with your pals if they merely use you as a sounding board for their complaints or if they actively work to prevent you from making any positive changes in your life. Don't be afraid to make adjustments in all areas of your life, including how much time you spend with particular friends. There will be people you learn from and maintain along the way to realizing your dreams, as well as those you learn from and let go.

5. **Set Aside Time For Self-Improvement**:
When people stop learning, they tend to become stagnant in all facets of their lives. Choose a new skill to master. Choose something you've always wished to learn to do, such as learning to play an

instrument or speak a different language. Take this time to focus on yourself and keep in mind that you are capable of learning new things and developing personally. People frequently lose sight of their potential when life and external factors appear to be against them. It's simple to fall into a rut and struggle to get out of it, but making time for yourself and your personal development is an investment that will eventually pay off handsomely. You'll understand how easy it is to strive toward and accomplish your goals once you recognize how much you've already learned.

Top Ten Tips Successful People Do In Achieving Their Dreams.

1. They make goals and strive to achieve them.
2. They are reliable.
3. They get the most out of each activity.
4. They accept accountability for their existence.
5. They develop meaningful relationships.
6. They put in extraordinary effort.
7. They never quit.
8. They take the risk.
9. They value discipline and hard work.
10. They develop principles.

There are many problems in life, but you have two options: you may give in and let life drag you around, or you can decide to change your habits and start living the life you've always wanted. You may start and stay on the path to success by using these five straightforward strategies for realizing your objectives and manifesting your dreams.

Chapter 4: THE CASE FOR A PURPOSEFUL LEADERSHIP

At whatever level of your organization, it is difficult to discover leaders. A leader's special combination of charisma, vision and personal qualities entices others to follow them. They also display the other nine traits that served as the foundation for this article series.

But the majority of the time, as they demonstrate these leadership qualities and attributes, they turn into the person that other people want to follow—or even choose to follow, given the choice.

It's crucial to check that all five components of the leadership model are present when hiring a leader:

1. **Communicate your purpose, the purpose of those around you, and how it relates to the mission of the business:**

When hiring leaders, I used to inquire about the candidates' backgrounds, the talents they had honed over time, their career objectives, and whether or not they would be a suitable fit for the company. These seemed to be the most crucial factors.

I now invest more time in trying to comprehend a candidate's goals and calling. I enquire, "What motivates you? What gives you energy?"

2. **Clearly define your position as a leader:**

It served as a useful reminder that a leader's primary responsibility is to release what I like to refer to as "human magic" by cultivating an atmosphere in which everyone is motivated and capable of giving their all. This includes building momentum and energy, especially in difficult situations. To assist others in seeing opportunities and potential. Creating vigor, inspiration, and hope is crucial to the job of a purposeful leader, yet thirty years ago I would have laughed this idea off.

3. **Identify your clients clearly**:

Some businesspeople believe that listening to their ego and using their sharp elbows can advance their careers. But are you interested in being someone like that? "The best leaders are hoisted to the summit; they do not climb to it. And that's how it happens: by helping others. "As a leader, you must support the team members who are running the company. You provide for your coworkers. You support the directors on your board. In order to best support those around you, you must first understand what they need to give of themselves.

4. **Be motivated by your values**:

On what is morally correct—honesty, respect, accountability, fairness, and compassion—we all generally agree. Every business appears to have admirable values. But if values only exist on paper, they are useless. Being motivated by values is acting morally—not only knowing or declaring what is right. It is a leader's responsibility to uphold these principles, actively promote them, and ensure that they permeate every aspect of the company.

5. **Be genuine; "Say what is true and do what is right."**

Be the best version of yourself—your truest, most complete self. Be frightened. Be genuine.

I once had the opinion that feelings should not be expressed in a professional setting. However, social connection is at the core of the business, and social connection is at the core of social connection. I had a lot to unlearn, and it took me a lifetime to accept the fifth, which is also the hardest for me personally.

LEADING STYLE

Changing behaviors is the best method to alter a company. Through employee interaction, communication, and decision-making, lean leadership promotes the creation of a culture of continuous improvement. This program will give you the tools, concepts, and coaching approaches you need to lead more effectively and efficiently inside your organization.

As leaders, we anticipate being led. In the absence of instructions, I will assume command, guide my team, and complete the task. I always act as a role model.

Effective Leadership Techniques

The majority of excellent leaders are passionate about developing and managing a top team. In any case, who wants to be the team leader of mediocrity and moderation? Who would that directly reflect negatively on? the executive. Leading exceptional teams, however, requires perseverance and the persistent pursuit of professional and personal growth.

1. **Develop a culture of leadership:**

There are many prosperous organizations where the highest-ranking executives are in no way in leadership. Although, They are in command. People also follow their instructions since they are authorities. However, those folks wouldn't adhere to them. On the other hand, there are certain persons at the very bottom of the totem pole who are the most effective leaders. Emerging leaders motivate those around them and take command in the lack of orders.

2. **Make the group feel secure**:
The team will exert every effort to carry out its duties and go above and beyond to aid in achieving corporate goals when they feel comfortable and supported.

Leadership and management are two distinct professions.

A team cannot be led into battle. You must guide them. It is difficult to imagine that anyone would feel secure during a battle. It all comes down to loyalty and trust. You feel overwhelmingly at ease when you can trust the team's leadership and the members to your right, left, and rear.

3. **Manage Actively Using Adaptive Change:**
Even if it means completely revamping your company, great leaders can recognize when change is necessary. The team may find this to be

frightening, and things frequently become worse before they get better.

The leadership must provide a few crucial items to manage change.

First, you must explain the change and why the business needs to remain successful.

Second, you must make sure that every team member, regardless of rank or position, is aware of how this change will affect them and what will be expected of them for it to be implemented successfully.

Thirdly, you must inform the team of the leadership's plans so that they may offer assistance and support during the period of transitional change.

Finally, throughout this time, communicate excessively and frequently and solicit feedback. "Pass the word," as we say in the SEAL teams. Simply put, this means explaining the situation to me. Make sure to explain everything to your staff.

4. **Offer your team your service**:
The idea of servant leadership is one that great leaders embrace. They never ask their staff to do anything that they haven't previously done or aren't willing to undertake themselves. Even while you can't always work side by side with your colleagues, making an effort to do so occasionally can be quite

helpful. When you're out there in charge, they will know that you remain concerned about their contributions to realizing the company's mission.

5. **Constantly eat last**:

Traditionally, when it's chow time, officers in the military eat last. This is a straightforward yet significant act of leadership. Your team will sacrifice for you if you make a sacrifice for them. The team is the one who must execute daily, so they must have the tools necessary to do so before you do.

Consistently putting these five aspects of leadership into practice is challenging. It demands regular concentration and effort. Ask yourself, "Am I being the best potential leader I can right now?" before each action and decision you take If not, change as necessary.

THE PURPOSEFUL LEADER

Leaders need to be extremely flexible and adaptable, able to negotiate complexity and ambiguity, given the rapid change and expansion that many firms are undergoing.

Lower employee turnover rates will result from making sure your staff members feel like they have a purpose.

"It's important to avoid concentrating on being reactive in daily activities. Create a strong organizational vision instead. When leaders are genuinely invested in this and involved in developing effective tactics to get there, purpose emerges.

Qualities of an Effective Leader

1. A leader that is attentive, genuine, and humble with high emotional intelligence.
2. A leader with a mindset that is adaptable and flexible
3. A leader that's willing to lead from a position of ethics, values, and mindfulness.
4. Clarity, control, and judgment.

5. An effective leader aligns the company's vision with the values of all stakeholders, including society and the environment
6. An effective leader thinks long-term rather than short-term

What sets a leader with a purpose apart from their less successful colleagues?

People immediately believe that being purposeful means sacrificing performance-driven behavior when you mention it.

An effective leader typically does the following:

1. **Inspire**: An effective leader typically inspires others around them in their shared vision.
2. **Engage**: He assigns each team member to worthwhile tasks.
3. **Innovate**: He creates new goods or methods.
4. **Achieve**: By establishing organization and clarity, he produces results.
5. **Develop**: He becomes more self-aware of their capacity to influence, coach, and alter others.